MYSTERIES UNCOVERED

Cities Lost to Time

by Craig Boutland

Gareth Stevens PUBLISHING

Published in 2027 by
Gareth Stevens Publishing
2544 Clinton St.
Buffalo, NY 14224

For Brown Bear Books Ltd:
Children's Publisher: Anne O'Daly
Design Manager: Keith Davis
Picture Manager: Sophie Mortimer

Picture Credits
Front Cover: Shutterstock: tenkl.
Interior: Dreamstime: Ali Rasool 11; iStock: 14, 19, 24, 26, 29, Digital Vision 15, Photos.com 8; Shutterstock: 4, 7, 16, Leonid Andronov 23, Maurice Arsene 20, Linda Bucklin 6, Shozib Ali Brohi 9, Roman Czupryniak 12, Sener Dagasan 13, Marino Denisenko 1, 5, Christin Echegaray 22, Angela Meier 18, muratart 21, Photo Magistr 17, Jo Reason 25, SL Photography 27, Wirestock Images 28.
All other artwork and Photography Brown Bear Books and Shutterstock.

Words in bold appear in the glossary on page 30.

Cataloging-in-Publication Data
Names: Boutland, Craig.
Title: Cities lost to time / Craig Boutland.
Description: Buffalo, NY : Gareth Stevens Publishing, 2027. |
Series: Mysteries uncovered | Includes glossary and index.
Identifiers: ISBN 9781482479096 (pbk.) | ISBN 9781482479102 (library bound) |
ISBN 9781482479119 (ebook)
Subjects: LCSH: Lost continents--Juvenile literature. | Extinct cities--Juvenile literature. |
Geographical myths--Juvenile literature. | Legends--Juvenile literature. |
Atlantis (Legendary place)--Juvenile literature.
Classification: LCC GN751.B68 2027 | DDC 398.234--dc23

Printed in the United States.

CPSIA compliance information: Batch #CS27GS: For further information contact Gareth Stevens at 1-800-542-2595.

Contents

INTRODUCTION

Lost cities are places where people used to live long ago but are now hidden or gone. Some sank underwater. Others were overgrown by plants. Around the world, dusty ruins are the reminders of once bustling cities that were home to thousands of people. This book explores the mysteries of lost cities, together with a lost island and a buried army of warriors. Why were they abandoned and how were they found again?

The Roman town of Pompeii was buried for 1,700 years by ash from a volcano.

Petra, in Jordan, was carved into rocky cliffs.

Forgotten Places

Some of these cities were trade centers. Others were places of political power or had religious significance. But they were all abandoned and then forgotten. They were overgrown by the jungle or buried beneath sand or ash. Some ruins lay undisturbed in rocky canyons or high on mountain peaks.

This book will take you from China to the Andes Mountains of Peru and from India to ancient Italy. You will read the remarkable stories of lost cities, their rediscovery, and how **archaeologists** uncovered their mysteries.

Sunken CITY

Atlantis is a legendary island that many people believe sank into the ocean. Some people believe it was a rich and powerful place with advanced technology. Others think it never actually existed.

Ancient stories say that Atlantis was a large island off the west coast of Europe. At its height, in around 9600 BCE, it was a powerful civilization.

The cities of Atlantis were destroyed when the island sank.

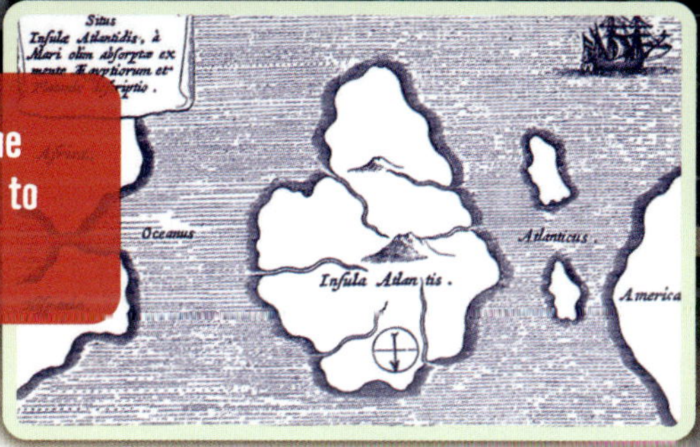

Some old maps of the Atlantic Ocean used to include Atlantis.

MYSTERY UNCOVERED

Ideas from Atlantis

Some people say that Atlantis helped spread new ideas across the world. That might explain why, for example, pyramids were built by ancient peoples in both Egypt and Mexico.

Atlantis was said to be bigger than Asia. Its people were wealthy and happy. But when ancient Greece defeated Atlantis, the island fell into **anarchy**. Its people became wicked and greedy for power. One legend tells that Atlantis sank to the bottom of the Atlantic Ocean after a huge earthquake hit the island.

No Evidence

Many people have looked for evidence that Atlantis once existed. No one has found any sign of it, even using high-tech tools like **sonar** to map the seabed. But there are still people who are convinced that the island once existed.

Mound of THE DEAD

In the 1920s, archaeologists heard about mysterious mounds of earth and bricks in an area in modern-day Pakistan. Beneath the mounds was an ancient city called Mohenjo-Daro. Its name means the Mound of the Dead.

A drain runs past a well and a wall in Mohenjo-Daro.

When archaeologists dug into the mound, they found the remains of one of the world's oldest cities. It had been buried 5,500 years before. The city was a capital of the civilization of the Indus Valley. The walls of another city called Harappa were nearby.

A Grid City

Mohenjo-Daro was built in about 3500 BCE around a strong **citadel**. The streets were laid out in a grid. Many of the homes had an upper floor with brick stairs. The residents of Mohenjo-Daro even had plumbing. Houses had their own bathrooms with drains.

MYSTERY UNCOVERED

Hit by Floods

Why were the Indus Valley cities abandoned? It was probably because they were hit by floods. Around the 18th century BCE, Mohenjo-Daro was flooded by both the Indus River and the Arabian Sea. The cities never recovered.

The homes were made from bricks of dried mud.

City of WONDERS

Babylon was once a powerful ancient city. It was said to be home to the Tower of Babel, which is mentioned in the Bible. It was also home to the Hanging Gardens, which were considered one of the Wonders of the World.

Babylon was at its most successful under King Nebuchadrezzar II (605–561 BCE). By then, the city had been the capital of Mesopotamia (present-day Iraq) for 3,000 years. It was also a trade center. But for some reason Babylon lost power and was abandoned.

A priest (at left) oversees the building of the Tower of Babel.

These are the remains of buildings from the ancient city.

MYSTERY UNCOVERED

A Gift for a Wife

Nebuchadrezzar may have built the gardens for his wife, because she missed the greenery and mountains of her homeland. The gardens had **terraces** and an irrigation system. They may have stood on a rooftop. All that remains today is a mound.

Tower of Babel

Nebuchadrezzar expanded the city on the banks of the Euphrates River. He built a great temple to a god named Marduk. Part of the temple was a stepped pyramid called a **ziggurat**. The pyramid might have been the basis for stories of the Tower of Babel, which was said to reach up to heaven.

Babylon's other famous construction was the Hanging Gardens. No one knows what the Hanging Gardens looked like, but they amazed everyone who saw them.

The Lost City of TROY

In the 7th or 8th century BCE, ancient Greek poet Homer wrote *The Iliad*. This famous poem described the destruction of the city of Troy. But was Troy a real place, or was the story just a myth?

The poem was popular for centuries, but no one was sure if its story was real. Then, in 1822, a British historian named Charles Maclaren suggested a likely site of Troy. He identified an **earthen** mound near the coast of what is now Türkiye. Local people called the place Hisarlik. Fifty years later, a German archaeologist, Heinrich Schliemann, confirmed that Maclaren was right.

In Homer's poem, the Greeks use a wooden horse to get inside Troy.

Layers and Layers

Schliemann and other experts found that nine cities had been built in the same place. As each city was abandoned, a new one was built on top. Homer's Troy was one of the oldest cities. It had a citadel and large houses. The walls had been destroyed by fire—just as Homer had described in his poem.

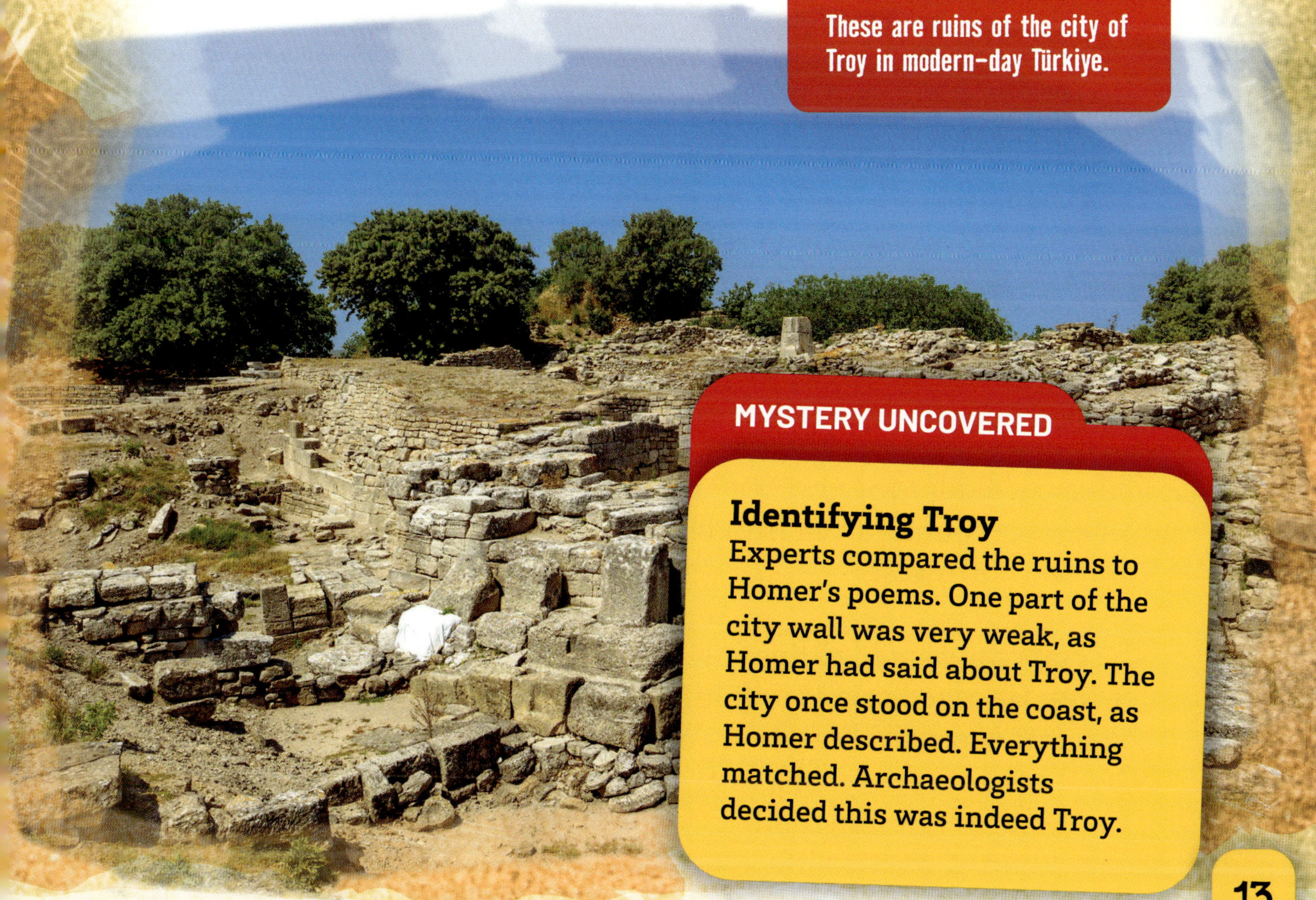

These are ruins of the city of Troy in modern-day Türkiye.

MYSTERY UNCOVERED

Identifying Troy

Experts compared the ruins to Homer's poems. One part of the city wall was very weak, as Homer had said about Troy. The city once stood on the coast, as Homer described. Everything matched. Archaeologists decided this was indeed Troy.

An Underground ARMY

In 1974, farmers in Xi'an, China, were digging a well. They found a 2,000-year-old tomb. The underground chamber covered 20 square miles (50 square km). It contained an army of thousands of clay soldiers.

The tomb belonged to China's first emperor, Qin Shi Huangdi. In the third century BCE, he united China and built the Great Wall to protect the country from invaders from the northwest.

The emperor wanted to live forever. He asked priests to find the secret of eternal life. He spent a lot of resources to build a vast, complex underground tomb to protect him in his next life.

Each warrior has its own facial expression and hairstyle.

The warriors are lined up in military formation.

Soldiers of Clay

The emperor ordered 700,000 men to build his tomb. They spent 36 years making 8,000 lifesized warriors out of **terracotta**. Each warrior is different, with unique facial features and different style of clothing. The soldiers carry real bronze weapons, including spears and crossbows. As well as soldiers, there were animals, chariots, and statues of entertainers. The tomb had everything the emperor would need in the next world.

MYSTERY UNCOVERED

Where Is the Emperor?

Despite finding the terracotta army, archaeologists found no sign of the emperor. They think a nearby mound might be his tomb. They haven't excavated it because it is said to contain mercury, which is a poisonous metal.

Buried by a VOLCANO

In 1748, a military engineer began to dig in a hillside near Naples in southern Italy. The site was near a volcano called Vesuvius. As the engineer dug, the earth fell away to reveal a city that had been buried 1,700 years earlier.

Victims were caught as they tried to escape.

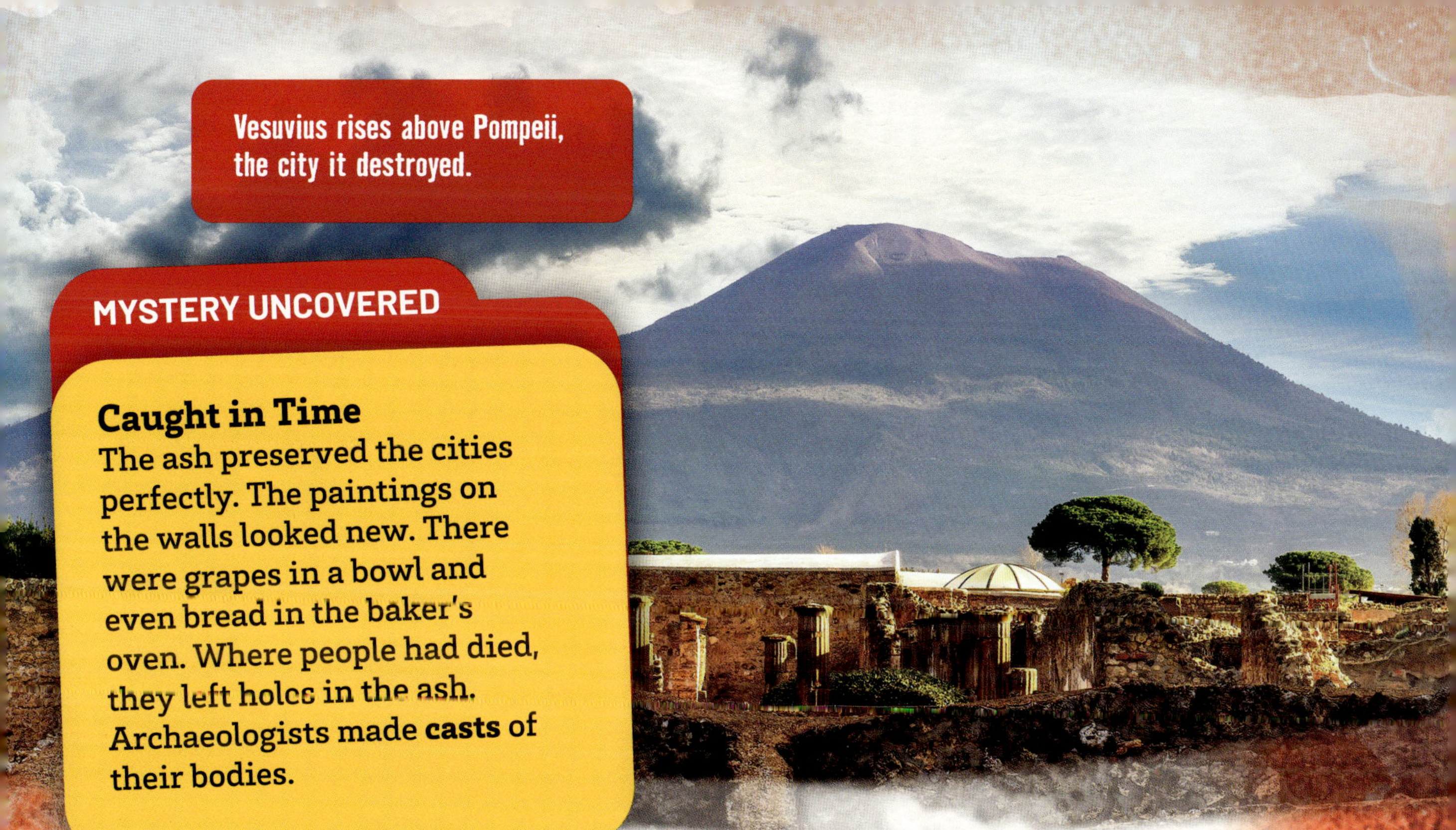

Vesuvius rises above Pompeii, the city it destroyed.

MYSTERY UNCOVERED

Caught in Time

The ash preserved the cities perfectly. The paintings on the walls looked new. There were grapes in a bowl and even bread in the baker's oven. Where people had died, they left holes in the ash. Archaeologists made **casts** of their bodies.

The city was Pompeii. It is now probably the most famous Roman city in the world. Pompeii was home to up to 20,000 people when Vesuvius **erupted** on August 24, 79 CE. Many people escaped, but thousands more were trapped as ash rained down, burying the town to a depth of 23 feet (7 m).

Preserved by the Ashes

Pompeii and Herculaneum, its neighbor, were completely buried. When the cities were rediscovered, they were perfectly preserved. Experts even found the shapes of people who had died as they tried to escape.

Hidden in ROCKS

In 1812, Swiss explorer Johann Burckhardt was traveling through southwest Jordan. He followed his guides through the twisting canyon of the Wadi Al-Siq. The rocky landscape gave no hint of what lay ahead. Burckhardt was astonished to see the remains of a secret city carved into the rose-pink rocks.

Petra could only be reached through a long, twisting gorge.

The hidden city was Petra. From the sixth century BCE to the second century CE, it was an important point on trade routes between Asia and Europe. The city was busy, with beautiful houses and gardens. The Nabataeans who lived there were wealthy. They carved buildings and tombs out of the sandstone cliffs. The people found a way to collect and distribute water. But in the end, the city fell into decline. Trade routes changed as it became easier to transport goods by sea. An earthquake in 363 CE destroyed the water supply and many of the buildings. The once powerful city was abandoned.

Many of the carved buildings in Petra were used as tombs.

MYSTERY UNCOVERED

Building in Rock

The Nabataeans were not the only people to carve buildings in rock. Lalibela, in Ethiopia, has rock-carved churches. Carving into hills was easier than cutting blocks of rock to use for building.

Temple in the JUNGLE

In 1860, French explorer Henri Mouhot was traveling in Cambodia, in Southeast Asia. In the middle of the jungle, he suddenly came across an amazing sight.

Mouhot found himself staring at huge stone faces that were smiling at him. The faces were carved on a ruined temple. There were more temples nearby. At the heart of the ruined city was the biggest temple of all: Angkor Wat.

These smiling faces appear on the Bayon Temple at Angkor in Cambodia.

The temples had been overgrown by huge trees.

MYSTERY UNCOVERED

Abandoned

In 1431, Angkor was invaded by its neighbors from Ayutthaya. They removed many treasures from the temples. Khmer power declined and so did the state religion. Most of the temples were abandoned. Angkor fell into ruins.

Capital of a Civilization

Angkor was the capital of the Khmer civilization from the 9th to the 15th centuries. Each new king built his own temple. Some were **Buddhist**, others were **Hindu**. Angkor Wat was built by King Suryavarman II in the 12th century. When the Khmers lost power, they abandoned the holy city and the jungle grew over the ruins.

City in the MOUNTAINS

Machu Picchu is an ancient city, high in the mountains of Peru. For hundreds of years, people outside the region didn't know it existed. In 1911, local farmers led American explorer Hiram Bingham to the site. Today, Machu Picchu attracts visitors from around the world.

The city was built by the Incas more than 500 years ago. The Incas had ruled a large **empire** in the Andes in the 15th century CE. When they were overthrown by the Spaniards in 1532, the Incas continued to live in cities hidden in the mountains. Machu Picchu has more than 150 stone buildings, including houses and temples. Terraces were cut into the mountainside for growing crops. Experts are unsure about the city's purpose. It may have been a royal palace. Or perhaps it had a religious purpose.

The Hitching Post of the Sun was used in religious ceremonies.

MYSTERY UNCOVERED

Sun Worship

The city has a short stone column called a hitching post. The column lines up with nearby peaks. Inca priests performed rituals there to "tie" the sun to Earth to stop the sun from moving too far away.

The city is among high mountain peaks.

Royal City of STONE

In Zimbabwe, in southern Africa, large stone walls on the plains mark the site of a lost city. The city had huge stone walls and towers and was once home to up to 20,000 people.

The "stone houses" are the remains of Great Zimbabwe. The Shona people built the city and lived there from the 11th to the 15th century. They raised cattle, grew crops, and traded gold. Their wealth was reflected in fine stone buildings. But then the city was abandoned.

The ruins of the city cover an area of 200 acres (80 ha).

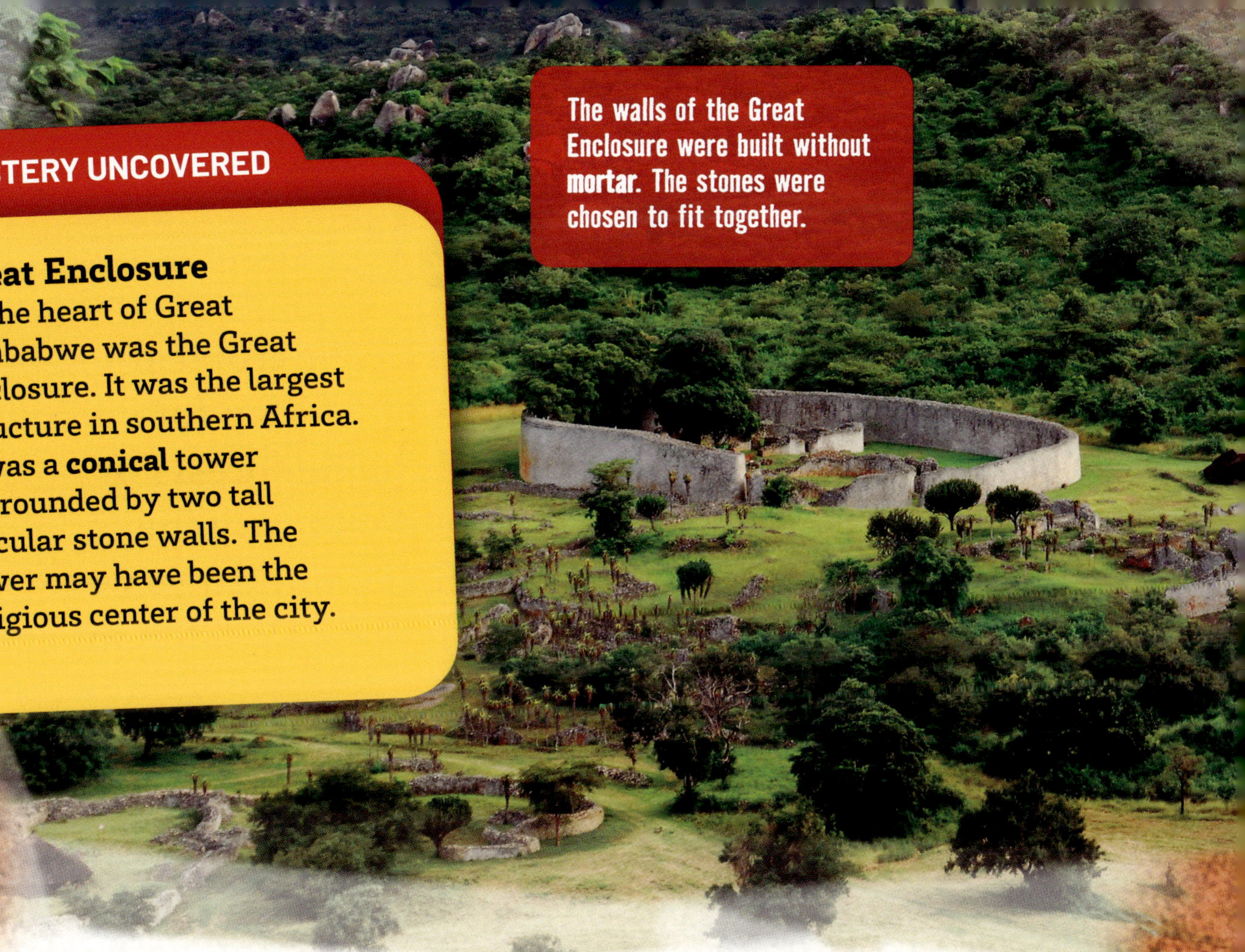

The walls of the Great Enclosure were built without **mortar**. The stones were chosen to fit together.

MYSTERY UNCOVERED

Great Enclosure

At the heart of Great Zimbabwe was the Great Enclosure. It was the largest structure in southern Africa. It was a **conical** tower surrounded by two tall circular stone walls. The tower may have been the religious center of the city.

Mystery Origin

European **colonists** saw the ruins of Great Zimbabwe in the 19th century. They were amazed by the sophisticated building techniques they found. That led them to conclude that an early European civilization must have built the city. It was not until the 20th century that archaeologists were finally able to prove that the city was built by Africans.

A Final Resting PLACE

The ruined city of Palenque lies in the tropical forests of southern Mexico. It was hidden for centuries. People began to explore the forests in the 19th century. In the mid–20th century the jungle was cleared and magnificent buildings were revealed. Most of the city still remains hidden in the thick foliage.

Pakal's tomb lay beneath the Temple of Inscriptions (left).

This carving shows Pakal in an elaborate royal headdress.

For around 300 years, from 600 to 900 CE, Palenque was an important city of the Mayans who ruled Mexico and Guatemala. The city's wealth was reflected in the high-quality of the carvings on its buildings.

MYSTERY UNCOVERED

Pakal the Builder

Inscriptions name Pakal as the main builder of Palenque. In 1952, archaeologist Alberto Ruiz Lhuillier found the king's tomb buried beneath the Temple of Inscriptions. Pakal's remains were covered in rich jade ornaments.

Magnificent Buildings

Most of the best buildings were constructed during the reign of Pakal the Great, from 615 to 683. The city had remarkable palaces, pyramids, and **aqueducts** to carry water. Palenque was abandoned near the end of the 10th century. The Maya probably fled after the city was invaded by enemies.

Birthplace of the GODS

When the Aztec came to power in Mexico, they found a ruined city of pyramids and palaces. The Aztec called the site Teotihuacán, which means "birthplace of the gods." They believed the universe was created there.

The Aztec made **pilgrimages** to the site. They were certain that this was where their own gods had created the sun. The main street was in the center of the city. It was known as the Avenue of the Dead and linked the two largest pyramids. These were the Pyramid of the Sun and the Pyramid of the Moon. Smaller pyramids lined the avenue.

Stone carvings decorated the temples.

Mexican City

Teotihuacán was built by an unknown people from Mexico in the first century BCE. It was a center for trade and crafts. The city was abandoned around 500 CE. It had some 200,000 citizens and covered an area of 8 square miles (20 square km). The city probably fell when war broke out among its rulers.

MYSTERY UNCOVERED

Sacrifices

In 2004, human skeletons were found beneath the Pyramid of the Moon. Were the people killed during the building process? Some early cultures in Mexico believed that human sacrifice was necessary to keep the gods happy.

The Pyramid of the Sun towers over the Avenue of the Dead.

GLOSSARY

anarchy A time when there is no law and order

aqueducts Artificial channels for carrying water

archaeologist Someone who studies objects from the past

Buddhist Someone who follows the religious teachings of the Buddha

casts Objects made by pouring liquid into molds to harden

citadel A strong fortification used for ruling a city

colonists People who settle in a new land that is controlled by their home country

conical In the shape of a cone that tapers to a blunt point

earthen Describes something made out of earth

empire A group of states with a single ruler, or emperor

erupted Exploded with great force

Hindu Someone who follows an ancient religion from India

inscriptions Words carved into stone as a permanent record

mortar Sticky substance used in buildings to hold stones or bricks together

pilgrimage Journeys to a sacred place or shrine

sonar A system that locates objects by bouncing sound waves off them

terraces Flat steps cut into the side of a hill

terracotta A kind of clay used for pottery and sculpture

ziggurat A form of pyramid built in a series of steps

FIND OUT MORE

Books

Cooke, Tim. *Pompeii and Other Legendary Ancient Places* (Ultimate Adventure Guides). Lerner Publications, 2024.

Doty, Abby. *Terra-Cotta Army* (Digging Up the Past). Northstar Editions, 2025.

Sonneborn, Scott. *Machu Picchu, Lost City of the Incas* (Investigating Mysterious Places). Capstone, 2025.

Websites

Machu Picchu
Britannica Kids' information about Machu Picchu
kids.britannica.com/kids/article/Machu-Picchu/346167

Top 10 Lost Cities
Listverse.com list of the famous lost cities
listverse.com/2011/09/09/top-10-lost-cities/

20 of the World's Lost Cities
Reader's Digest's descriptions of 20 great lost cities
www.rd.com/list/lost-cities/

INDEX